THREE STEPS TO SUCCESS

1.11.11

To all at Woodhouse,

Very best of luck in the future!

Best wishes

Ralph

Raphael Mokades is the managing director of Rare Recruitment, a firm that specialises in helping the most able new graduates from diverse backgrounds find the jobs that are right for them. Raphael grew up in London and is a graduate of Oxford University. On graduating he worked for the *Financial Times* for a year before taking responsibility for diversity policy at Pearson plc for a period of three years. He founded Rare Recruitment in 2005, and has helped hundreds of people find jobs with some of the best employers in the world, including Goldman Sachs, the Civil Service Fast Stream and L'Oréal.

THREE STEPS TO SUCCESS

Essential advice on how to maximise your chances in the graduate job market

RAPHAEL MOKADES

PROFILE BOOKS

First published in Great Britain in 2011 by
Profile Books Ltd
3a Exmouth House
Pine Street
Exmouth Market
London EC1R 0JH
www.profilebooks.com

10 9 8 7 6 5 4 3 2 1

A CIP catalogue record for this book is available from the British Library.

ISBN: 978 1 84668 517 0
eISBN: 978 1 84765 768 8

Designed and typeset in Stone Serif by sue@lambledesign.demon.co.uk
Printed and bound in Great Britain by Hobbs the Printers

FSC www.fsc.org MIX Paper from responsible sources FSC® C020438

CONTENTS

INTRODUCTION

Across the UK, more young people are going to university than ever before. Young people with passion, drive and ambition; young people with bravery, creativity and spark; young people who, if all were equal, would inherit the earth. And yet still huge numbers of young people study the wrong subject, and end up with either the wrong job or, worse, no job at all.

My motivation in writing this book is very simple: to help young people, and their parents, make the right choices about higher education and entry into the employment market. The issues I present are grounded in reality, and the solutions I suggest are based on the time-honoured principles of working hard and knowing how to play the game. Nothing I say is new or unique. I take no credit for setting down a series of truths which are probably self-evident. But I hope that I can present these truths in a clear and helpful way.

Bucking the bling: aiming for real and lasting success

I start by defining the success I talk about – *real and lasting success*. We're not talking about Andy Warhol's 'fifteen minutes of fame' – about getting on to a reality television show, becoming a rapper with a hit single, or a professional footballer for a few years. Of course, some people are lucky enough to have the breaks to do this, and are savvy enough to make a career out of it – but success of this sort cannot be guaranteed. More modest, pedestrian, solid successes can, by contrast, be pretty much guaranteed – if you work hard enough and in the right direction.

So when I talk about real and lasting success, I mean forgetting the 'I want it now' attitude, bucking the 'bling', and formulating and executing long-term strategies that will lead to professional and financial security by the age of forty.

Becoming a strategist

Recent research by Queen Mary, University of London classified young job seekers into four categories:[1]

- **Disillusioned** – People whose experience of education and the labour market has been negative and who believe that conventional career structures have nothing to offer them.

1 G. Healy, H. Bradley and C. Williams, *Making Career Choices: The Experiences of Young Black and Minority Ethnic People Entering the Labour Market*, Centre for Research in Equality and Diversity, School of Business and Management, Queen Mary, University of London, 2006.

- **Cynics** – People who do have some conventional ambitions, but who doubt very much that they themselves will be able to succeed.

- **Hard Workers** – People who believe that they will advance if they keep their heads down, work hard, and take the opportunities they are offered.

- **Strategists** – People who work hard and believe that avenues are open to them, but who do more than just wait for opportunities to come to them. Strategists work out what they want to do, and how to get there, and then actively pursue opportunities. They understand that there will be obstacles – including, for example, racism – in their way, but are determined to find a way to navigate round them. In short, they have a detailed and realistic idea of how to achieve real and lasting success.

Put yourself, for one minute, in the shoes of an employer. You interview four candidates.

The first is dressed in a slovenly way, gives monosyllabic answers, and displays no enthusiasm for the job – after all, this person is **Disillusioned** and thinks everyone is out to get him, so there's no point in making any effort. Indeed, he's only coming to the interview to keep his mother (or employment adviser) happy.

The second interviewee is a **Cynic**. This person is smartly dressed and seems to want the job, but asks a load of questions that you perceive to be aggressive and untrusting. Can she join a union? How many women and black people are there in senior management? What is the pay? When will she be able to renegotiate it? What are the working hours like? Is there paid overtime? What is the grievance procedure if she feels she is passed over for promotion? She doesn't ask much about the work, or show you that she is right for the job – instead, she makes you feel as if you're on trial and that she's concerned that she won't be treated fairly.

Next comes the **Hard Worker**. This person, again, is well dressed and enthusiastic, but gives no signs of being troublesome. When asked to talk about his strengths, he stresses his commitment, ability to work long hours, technical skills, and interest in climbing the career ladder. He's applied to lots of organisations and doesn't seem too bothered about which one he ends up working for – he just wants a good, solid job with security, and in return he'll work hard.

And finally, in comes the **Strategist**. Unlike the Cynic, she doesn't ask a load of aggressive questions – but like the Cynic, she has thought about them. The difference is that she has been clever enough to contact a friend of a friend who already works for the firm and has asked her all these questions first. She's done her due diligence (and indeed has pulled out of job interviews after this stage in the past). In fact, she's done loads of research – and you, the interviewer, are wowed by her understanding of your industry, your organisation and its culture. She's applied for a few positions, not many, and tells you that you are her first choice. You believe her. She's impeccably well dressed, polite and enthusiastic – totally professional – but she's more than that. When asked to talk about her strengths, she stresses her creativity and resourcefulness – and backs this up with solid examples.

You come to sum up. The Disillusioned guy didn't seem to want the job, and the Cynic seemed aggressive and confrontational – in short, like nothing but trouble. You're sure the Hard Worker would give you years of loyal service, but the Strategist would give you this, and more. You're really excited about the prospect of having her work for you – and besides, she seems to really want the job. You hire the Strategist.

The goal of this book is to turn people into strategists. Before becoming a strategist, you need to do three things. First, you need to begin believing in yourself, and in your ability to achieve your goals. Second, you need to take control of your destiny, by setting those goals after some serious thinking. And third, you need to learn the rules of the game, the game you'll need to play to get what you want. Once you've done all this – once you're confident and clued up, full of self-belief and direction – then you'll have become a true strategist.

STEP 1

BELIEVE IN YOURSELF

Leave the doubt at the door

Self-belief is crucial in achieving real and lasting success. Obstacles will inevitably present themselves during the course of your education and career: the question is whether you allow them to defeat you, or whether you find ways to overcome them. When you go into an interview, you have to be able to Leave the Doubt at the Door – and convey a sense of total confidence in your own abilities. This chapter is about how to do that. Remember the Disillusioned person and the Cynic? Neither of them has confidence in their own ability to transcend problems – and as a result, neither will get hired.

Dealing with the fear of failure

At some point, you'll fail.

That's inevitable.

It might be an exam, a driving test or a job interview. It might be absolute – an X in an A-level paper, a first-round rejection from a job you really wanted; or it might be relative – a 2:2 when you wanted a 2:1, or a final-round rejection with flattering feedback from that job. But trust me – at some point, you'll fail, and it'll be horrible.

What defines you is not that you fail – that simply makes you human – but how you deal with it. *You* decide whether or not to let it defeat you. No matter how extreme or crushing the circumstance, there is always a way back. As John D. Rockefeller put it, 'I always tried to turn every disaster into an opportunity.'

Consider these two examples.

According to the Bible, Joseph was the overconfident youngest son of Jacob. Of Jacob's ten sons he was known as the favourite. His older brothers conspired against him and sold him to slave traders, while telling their father that he was eaten by a lion. Joseph saw God's plan for his life in his dreams; so he endured his sufferings with confidence and strength.

The slavers took Joseph to Egypt and sold him to one of the pharaoh's officers. Joseph served his master well and gained his favour. But the master's wife tried to seduce Joseph, even though he was a young man of impeccable integrity. After he rejected her, she made false accusations about him to her husband. Joseph was thrown in prison. The prison guard befriended him and learned of Joseph's divinely inspired talent for interpreting dreams.

Because of this reputation, Joseph was called by the pharaoh to interpret a dream that deeply troubled him. None of the pharaoh's advisers could decipher it. Joseph accurately related the symbols in the dream to a future time of abundance that would be followed by a time of great famine.

The pharaoh rewarded Joseph by making him the governor of the lands of Egypt. During the prosperous times he stored up the plentiful harvest, planning for the future. During the years of famine, Joseph's brothers came to Egypt in search of grain and food to keep their people from starving. They did not recognise him in this prominent Egyptian noble. He ordered them to return with their younger brother. When they returned with Benjamin, Joseph revealed his identity. The brothers expressed great remorse for their actions. Joseph forgave them. He and his grieving father enjoyed a joyous reunion. Joseph's years of steadfast reliance on God brought about not only the reunion but his high status, and he was able to save his nation from starvation.

If that tale is a little too far back in time for your taste, consider a more recent example. The racist apartheid regime in South Africa subjugated that country's black population in a brutal and repressive fashion, denying black people the vote, forbidding marriage between members of different races, and stipulating where different races could live. The regime was armed to the teeth, the black population generally ill educated and unarmed. The struggle to bring freedom to black South Africans was led by Nelson Mandela, who describes his life in his autobiography, *Long Walk to Freedom*. In 1962 Mandela was captured, and imprisoned on Robben Island, a bleak, windswept outcrop at the very bottom of the African continent. Mandela was subject to solitary confinement for 18 of his 27 years in prison, and was the victim of countless attempts to break his spirit – the cruelty of the guards, backbreaking hard labour, and being forced to sleep in tiny, barely habitable cells.

And yet Mandela stayed strong. In his autobiography, he

explains how. He didn't consider himself hopeless in the face of white oppression; he found strength from within, overcame every obstacle in his path, and eventually, in 1994, became the first president of a free South Africa.

The blunt truth is that if Nelson Mandela could survive eighteen years in solitary confinement with his spirit unbroken, then any – *any* – hardship or disadvantage faced by a young person in the UK today can also be overcome. I'm not suggesting that it'll be easy (it won't be), or that the playing field between you and the most privileged in society will be level (it won't be). But with the right preparation and sufficient determination, you can achieve real and lasting success. You cannot control exactly what happens to you – but you can, and must, control how you react. You decide whether to be the victim of your circumstances, or whether to conquer them.

Being a victim – and three ways to prevent it

A variant of being terrified of failure is to believe that it's been impossible for you to succeed in the first place. People with this mindset will assert that owing to the school they attended, their family circumstances, the colour of their skin, or other factors, it's impossible for them to achieve real and lasting success.

As already stated, such circumstances are all real and they all impact on individuals. But, once again, it's up to us to decide exactly how they impact on us personally. Here are three suggestions for how to overcome the feeling of being a victim.

1. **Voluntary work.** If you're feeling really terrible about your own circumstances, one of the most uplifting things you can do is to help other people whose situations may be even more desperate than yours. Working in a hospice with people who are dying, with disabled children, with victims of domestic violence, with refugees – this kind of work does three things. One: it helps you realise that your own situation is not uniquely terrible, and that there are people worse off than you. Two: it makes you feel useful and powerful – you have the power to help someone else. And three: it improves your personal brand, of which more later.

2. **Inspiring stories**. Reading *A Long Walk to Freedom* by Mandela, or the writings of Martin Luther King or Mahatma Gandhi, or the Bible stories, or the autobiographies of figures you especially admire – whatever it is, you can draw strength from the stories of others who have drawn triumph from tragedy. If they can do it, so can you – and you need to keep reminding yourself of this.

3. **Mentoring.** Finally, you should seriously consider getting a mentor. If there is someone you especially admire – especially someone who perhaps shares some of the characteristics that you feel make you a victim – then seek them out, and ask them whether they will be your mentor. It's probably smartest to go for someone relatively unknown and available – perhaps the guy from your school who, unusually, did make it to uni, or the girl you know who was in care but still got a great job as a lawyer – rather than an MP or pop star, who is likely to be

inundated with such requests. Do *not* be shy of asking – in our experience, the vast majority of people who are asked to mentor are deeply flattered, and say yes. *Do*, however, set clear guidelines for the relationship – what each of you should expect, how long the mentoring will last in total, how often you will meet, etc.

The Mentoring & Befriending Foundation has a wealth of information on how to find a mentor: http://www.mandbf.org.uk/getinvolved/individual/find_a_mentor_or_befriender/

STEP 2

TAKE CONTROL

Own your own destiny

Imagine a man armed with a map of London, walking around, looking for Waterloo Bridge. His map is up to date, he has left plenty of time, and he is looking very hard indeed. He just can't seem to find Waterloo Bridge, though. Why not?

Because he's in Glasgow.

No matter how hard he looks, he won't find Waterloo Bridge. He could buy a bigger map, with more detail. He could ask passers-by. He could even climb a tall building to get a better view. But he won't find Waterloo Bridge – because he's in the wrong city.

Sound ridiculous? Yes – and no. I have met dozens of young people, Hard Workers, who are convinced that hard work alone will bring them real and lasting success. But like the man in Glasgow looking for Waterloo Bridge, they've got the wrong map.

Before you start working hard, you need to think, hard, about what you want, and what you need to do to get there. I'll go through the details of executing your strategy in a subsequent chapter – but for the moment, assume you can do anything you want once you know just what your goals are. The aim of this chapter is to help you set those goals.

Matching your goals to your personality

Before you start to think about what you might want to do, you need to know yourself. We're not talking spiritual enlightenment here – what I mean by this is that you need to know what is really important to you in a job. People often fail to consider these cultural factors, and end up unhappy, not because the work they are doing fails to interest them, but because of the working hours, or the travel, or the drinking culture.

So, here's a suggestion. This might take a while, and some people find it quite difficult as an exercise. But I strongly suggest that you do it. Take a blank sheet of paper and draw a line down the middle of it. On the left-hand side, write down all the times in your life you can think of when you've been really happy. On the right-hand side, write down all the unhappy occasions.

Now, look at your list. Look for trends. What really, really makes you happy? Is it working with a group of great people? Is it order, structure, and routine? Is it having a fantastic teacher and meaningful learning experiences? Is it material success, or the respect of your peers? And what makes you unhappy? Is it working too many hours? Being shouted at? Feeling undervalued? Being underpaid? Feeling lonely?

This list is a window into your character. When choosing a career, you need to pick a route that will allow you to be happy. If you hate high-pressured, aggressive environments, then you do not want a career in such an environment. If you value material success above all else, then you shouldn't pick a career that pays badly. It sounds hugely obvious, and it is – but most people never do this and so end up in a career to which they are fundamentally badly suited.

Once you know your own priorities, the next step is to do your research into the companies and industries that interest you. You need to do this fundamental research *before* you go for interview. By far the best way is to use your personal network to talk to someone already working for the firm that interests you, and to ask him or her, informally, what it's like to work there. Failing that, you can read brochures, critical websites like Vault, and attend open days.

Here, for starters, are some general points about the cultures of different industries.

Drinking culture

In some firms and some industries, it's expected that you'll spend a good deal of time drinking with colleagues and clients. I have never heard of anyone being forced to drink, but what I'm talking about is being prepared to spend large amounts of time around booze and with people who are drunk. The most extreme case here is the advertising industry – most agencies have a bar inside the building. Other professions where you are likely to have to be around alcohol are event management, PR, the sales divisions of investment banks, and commercial law firms.

Working hours

I have lost count of the number of people I know who have got 'good' jobs, say with a top commercial law firm, and who, a year into their careers, say, 'It's all right but I can't stand the hours.' What did they expect? The truth of the matter is that many – perhaps most – really desirable jobs come with brutal working hours attached. Commercial law involves very long hours. So does working in the mergers and acquisitions area of an investment bank. So does most strategy and management consultancy. So does the audit function in accountancy, at least during 'audit season'.

The jobs where the hours are most reasonable are those in the public sector, in some charity and media jobs (especially telesales), in management consultancy serving the public sector, in the tax function of the big accountancy firms, and in major FTSE companies with good work-life policies.

Training

Some people are happy to learn as they go. Others desperately want structured training. Some sales organisations give fantastic training, and if you take a human resources or marketing job you may be offered the chance to study for a Chartered Institute of Personnel and Development (CIPD) or Chartered Institute of Marketing (CIM) qualification. If you become a lawyer or an accountant you will get structured training leading to a qualification. Some big FTSE companies also give excellent training, and so do many investment banks. The areas where you may not be trained as well are: some less reputable sales jobs; publishing, journalism, advertising, and public relations; some retail and manufacturing companies.

Travel

Some jobs will see you go into the same office, day after day after day. Others will see you constantly on the road. Strategy consulting, certain types of journalism and field sales will necessarily mean travelling around. By contrast, banking, law, some accountancy (not audit) and many public sector jobs will entail going to the same office day after day.

Numbers

This sounds really obvious, but again, it's worth spelling out. If you love maths and numbers, then a job in a bank or an accountancy firm, or in the finance function of any other organisation, is a good idea. If you can't stand numbers, then it isn't.

Words

Again really obvious, but again frequently ignored. If you love to write and play with words, then law, journalism, publishing and public relations are obvious destinations.

Routine

If you crave a job with order and a predictable schedule, then make sure you go into the right field. Much public sector work, the tax function in accountancy, and trading in a bank all produce days and weeks with relatively consistent patterns.

Selling

If you love to sell, then do it for a job! Companies *always* need good salespeople. Media companies sell advertising space; consumer goods companies sell consumer products; banks sell financial products. In general, salespeople tend to earn well and have to work less brutal hours. Don't be misled by the popular image of the double-glazing salesman – selling a reputable product for a reputable company is a great thing to do and a surefire way to start your career: if you can make your company money, your company will value you.

Talking to people

If you love nothing more than forging relationships, persuading people to do things and building networks, then think about public relations, journalism or sales.

Helping people

Some people are primarily driven by the opportunity to help others. This might mean working in the not-for-profit or public sectors, helping the less fortunate in society. But it might also mean supporting customers – giving people fantastic service and helping them get what they want. This is what commercial lawyers, tax accountants and bankers working in mergers and acquisitions do – so if part of your motivation is to help people, don't think that you necessarily have to look away from the business world.

Initial choices

So, you have got to know yourself a little better and you have some idea of what you might want to do. What do you need to do to get there in terms of initial choices?

This is where the vast majority of people go wrong. There are a number of pernicious myths that contribute to this failure. The truth is that most employers are looking for similar things – and that these myths represent pretty much the opposite of what they're looking for. So, here they are, these six myths that need shattering – and the truth about what employers really want.

Myth 1: Work hard, keep your head down, and you'll be all right

This is absolute nonsense. Working hard is necessary, but it's not sufficient. Something like 30 per cent of young people now have a degree, or more than one degree – and having qualifications just does not mark you out any more. You need to think about building your personal brand – about being a strategist, not just a hard worker – and about making your CV impressive by dint of achievements outside academia.

Myth 2: Everyone has a first degree now – you need a master's degree to make yourself stand out

No, no, no, no, no. No. Absolutely not. Having more than one degree absolutely does not make you more employable in general. This is maybe the worst myth of all. If you have a clear idea of what you want to do, and you know for a fact that you need an extra qualification to do it – for example, a master's in economics to work for the Bank of England – then that's a different story, but for most mainstream employers a seemingly randomly chosen master's degree will have the opposite effect to what you want. It'll make you look indecisive, and as if you didn't have a clear career plan – like a Hard Worker rather than a Strategist. It'll put you deeper into debt. And (unlike in America) it won't even guarantee you a higher starting level of pay – UK employers usually pay people with and without postgraduate qualifications exactly the same starting rate. Far better, in short, to save the eight or ten grand and plunge into the labour market a year earlier, having thought really hard about what you want to do.

Myth 3: You should do something vocational (i.e. related to your likely future career) – study law!

Here is the truth. What you study at university doesn't really matter. Let me repeat that. *What you study at university doesn't really matter.* Almost all employers hire new graduates on the basis that they're looking for talent, and on the understanding that knowledge can be taught later. In fact, most top employers probably have a prejudice *against* the so-called vocational subjects. My advice to you – in the strongest possible terms – is to study what you enjoy. Apparently 'useless' degrees like English literature, history and classics are actually excellent choices, because they teach useful skills – such as the ability to synthesise large amounts of information from reading lists, and to produce arguments in essays.

So, to be specific, here are some 'vocational' versus 'academic' routes to think about:

Q: *I want to be a lawyer. Should I do history or law?*

A: You should do whatever you enjoy more, but bear in mind that many people who do law degrees find them quite boring. Should you choose to do a history degree, you will have to do a one-year conversion course to law (the Graduate Diploma in Law) – but if you get a training contract with a solicitor's firm (or, in some cases, a pupillage with a barristers' chambers), they'll pay for this.

Q: *I want to be an accountant. Should I do accounting or economics?*

A: Economics. It will give you a broader perspective, and to qualify as an accountant you'll have to gain a professional qualification (ACCA or CIMA) once you join your firm anyway. Having an accounting degree won't put you at any advantage.

Q: *I want to be a journalist. Should I do English literature or media studies?*

A: You should probably do English literature. Media studies has an unfortunate reputation as a course studied at the least prestigious universities by the least able students. The media can be extremely snobbish and what counts is your ability to network and charm people – and you'll probably have a better chance of doing this if you've studied the same thing as the people you're trying to charm, and gone to the same sort of university as them.

Q: I'm interested in business. I like figures. Should I study maths or business studies?

A: Definitely go for maths. Maths graduates have the highest chance of being employed after graduation, and mathematical ability is becoming more and more commercially valuable. In addition, business studies has something of the same reputational problem as media studies.

Myth 4: No one's going to be impressed that you worked in McDonald's. Don't put that on your CV

Work experience matters. Faced with two candidates with identical academic records, we can guarantee you that employers will look to see which of them has done more (and more meaningful) work experience. Meaningful experience does not necessarily mean shadowing someone's mum for a week – it can mean having the discipline to stick at a difficult, boring job for a significant period of time. And yes, that includes McDonald's. If you have worked in the same place for a couple of years, that suggests you're reliable – you turn up for work, and on time – you're honest, and you're competent. Those are precisely the kinds of things employers need to see. So make sure you know the value of your work experience – there's more on presenting your experience in interviews and more on CVs in the next chapter.

Myth 5: Stop wasting time with this football/music/ community work – it'll detract from your work and employers aren't interested in it

Oh yes they are. Let's pretend you're the interviewer again.

Imagine two candidates with identical academic records and very similar work experience. One has not done anything except study and work. The other has set up a football team, recruited players, and joined a league. You interview both. The first has little to say outside his work and academic experience. The second is bubbling with enthusiasm for his team – and, as it happens, you rather like football too.

Who do you hire?

Myth 6: You need a secure job – job security is the most important thing

It depends what you want, of course, but in general I would suggest that this isn't a very smart or a very strategic approach. It tends to be the case that with the best-paid jobs there is an element of risk. In investment banking, for example, industry downturns can lead to swathes of lay-offs. But with a lay-off comes a financial pay-off, and the industry usually picks up again before long. If you're prepared to tolerate a degree of uncertainty, you'll probably end up with a more interesting career and more money.

STEP 3

LEARN THE RULES

If you want to play at Wimbledon, you've got to wear white

In the late 1980s a new tennis prodigy hit the scene. Andre Agassi was a showman – a Las Vegan of Iranian extraction famous for hitting the ball between his legs, having long, dyed hair, earrings, and the most outrageous combinations of clothing – pink cycling shorts worn underneath black tennis shorts was a particular favourite. Agassi made his name on the hard courts of the United States, and in the summer of 1991 he was finally ready to make his Wimbledon debut.

The All England Club, which runs Wimbledon, stipulates that players' dress must be predominantly white. And the All England Club was not about to relax this rule for a hairy Las Vegan. The press speculated feverishly about what Agassi would do – would he flout the dress code completely? Or wear something outrageous but just about predominantly white?

What Agassi did, of course, was to confound expectations and appear dressed entirely in white – white shoes, white socks, white shorts and white shirt. Asked about his attire in the subsequent press conference, Agassi made the simple point – this was the All England Club, not the Agassi club, and these were their rules. He couldn't expect them to change them just for him. The rest, of course, is history: Agassi went on to win the Wimbledon title in 1992, became one of the few men in history to win all four Grand Slam tournaments, shaved his head and ended up becoming one of the game's elder statesmen.

What, you may ask, has this got to do with getting a great job? More than you might think. Because the fundamental issue is the same – no matter how driven and able you are, *if you don't play by the rules, you won't be allowed in.* You need to know the rules of the game. Once you have the self-belief and the strategy, it's a question of tactics – you need to learn how to present yourself in the light that makes you desirable to employers.

That is the goal of this chapter – to show you how to play the game and present yourself right.

CVs

Imagine you are a recruiter sifting through a couple of hundred CVs. You're going to interview about twenty people, invite about six to an assessment centre, and finally hire two. Let's imagine this is for a fairly standard graduate job and they have set the usual criteria.

The first thing you'll do is exclude all the CVs that blatantly don't meet the criteria – for example, people who have failed to make the required grades, or who don't have the right to work in the UK.

But this still leaves you with 150-odd CVs, all of which

meet your minimum criteria – and you need to get these down to twenty. What next?

You look at the CVs again. Some of them have spelling mistakes, grammatical errors. Most don't. Remember, you need to get that pile of 150 down to twenty-odd. You can get a person who meets all your criteria and who has taken the trouble to check his or her spelling and grammar – or one who hasn't. What do you do?

You can get 150 down to 130 by eliminating people for being slack, careless and disrespectful of your time. You do it.

Now you have 130 people – all of whom can spell and punctuate, and all of whom meet your criteria. So you start to assess them. Academically, the candidates are all much of a muchness – they're all good enough. So you look at their work experience section and you look at the extra-curricular activities. What attracts you?

Candidates who have done stuff, who have got involved, who have been leaders and team players and who have worked and understand the discipline required in a professional environment. Quite a lot of the applicants appear never to have done a day's paid work in their lives, so you bin them – you don't want to be the first to risk it. (Of course, it may be that they have worked but haven't put the work on their CVs because they think it 'unimpressive' – but you don't know that.) Quite a lot more seem not to have done anything except work or study. So you bin them, too. That takes you down to 40 – you're closing in on your target of 20 now.

You've got 40 CVs of people with good work experience, good extra-curricular activities, solid academic experience and an ability to spell and punctuate. So now, you ask: do they really want to do the job? Is their work or extra-curricular experience relevant? Do they illustrate the kinds of values or competencies that your organisation really values?

There are lots of impressive candidates here, and about 25 or so have clearly researched the company and have personalised their CVs for this particular application. The way they describe their work and extra-curricular experience clearly shows that they have the kinds of skills and values you're looking for. There really isn't much to choose between these 25 on content alone. Most of the CVs are beautiful too – nicely laid out with loads of white space, uncluttered, and easy to read. One or two are real dog's breakfasts, though – people fiddling with the margins to cram too much information on to the page, using type which is too small to read easily, having loads of fonts all on the same page. You ask yourself why you should be working hard to read these illegible CVs – and decide you shouldn't. So you bin the five CVs that were less easy on the eye – and you've reached your 20.

Key lessons: perfecting your CV

That may give some context for how recruiters look at CVs. Here's a checklist which should be easy to follow:

1. Get the presentation right. Specifically:

- **Spelling and grammar** – check them, get someone else to check them, and then double-check them. A spelling error is almost certainly going to result in your CV getting binned.

- **Font size** – use 11 or 12 point for text. Don't use more, don't use less. It won't do you any favours. You can vary the size for headings.
- **Font type** – you can use a *serif* font (like Times) or a *sans serif* (like Arial) – it doesn't matter. What does matter, however, is that you **use the same font throughout**. Use bold and vary the font size, but steer clear of underlining and italics.
- **Margins** – don't fiddle with them. If what you want to say doesn't fit on to the page, it's too much, so reduce it.
- **Length** – two pages **maximum**. Again, more than this suggests you have a problem being succinct.
- **Layout** – ensure plenty of white space between sections. Don't use tables. Make sure your name is at the top of the CV and make sure it's in a large font.
- Contact details – give one email address and one telephone number, and make sure the address is one you check regularly. Do not allow your email account to go over quota or your phone to run out of credit – the result, very simply, is that the employer won't be able to get hold of you and will go to another candidate who is easier to contact. If your contact details change, make sure that you tell any organisations you've applied to straight away. And use a businesslike email address. Sexyplaya89@hotmail.com does not look good.

This stuff is really basic – but people slip up on it very frequently, and as a result don't even get called for interview. Don't be one of those people.

2. Work experience

You need to harness your work experience as a tool that enables you to present yourself in the best possible light. Ideally, your work experience section should:

- Illustrate that you have a track record of turning up for work, including boring and mundane work, and taking orders.
- Show that you are ambitious and competent – this is where a couple of weeks' work shadowing at an impressive firm can be good.
- Demonstrate your interest in the field – if you want to be a lawyer, you should aim to do some work experience in a legal environment; if you want to be a journalist, a couple of weeks with your local paper, etc.
- Prove that you are successful in what you do – i.e. if you do a part-time telesales job, you should quantify how often you hit or exceed target and how much revenue you have brought in.

3. Extra-curricular activities

Just like work experience, your extra-curricular activities need to be harnessed for maximum impact. The perfect extra-curricular section would:

- Show evidence of your ability to be self-starting and creative – for example, starting your own business or a new society at university.

- Illustrate your personal impact – you should quantify, for example, the number of members in a society you run or the amount of money your business made.
- Show that you are a team player – evidence of helping out, perhaps in a community or voluntary capacity.
- Reinforce your interest in the job at hand – so if you are interested in banking, perhaps you have been involved in a student investment society.

4. Passion

As a recruiter, when you see a CV that bubbles with passion for your company, you inevitably put the candidate into the 'yes' pile. Making your CV passionate is not easy, but the key lies in showing that your experiences of work and of extra-curricular activity resonate with the interests and values necessary to pursue a career in the company you are applying to.

5. Personalisation

Like people, organisations have personalities, and it will be obvious by now that the best way to make yourself appealing to an employer is to make your CV personalised.

Of course, this takes time and effort, and it's not realistic to send off hundreds of carefully personalised CVs.

But here is the beautiful thing – **you don't need to**. You believe in yourself. You know yourself. You're only applying for things you really want to do, and which are right for you. You should make, at most, a dozen carefully targeted applications.

For an example of a killer CV, **see Appendix 1**.

Competency-based application forms

Some companies use competency-based application forms instead of CVs. This means that instead of asking for a CV, you'll fill out an online form with your personal details, exam results, etc., and then answer a few questions – for example, 'Give an example of a time when you had to work hard to influence people. What was the result?'

This is basically asking for your CV, but in another way. The essential thing with these application forms is to recognise that they want you to answer the questions *with examples from a variety of areas*. It's up to you to give examples from your academic life, your extra-curricular activities and your work experience – and to give a good variety. This way, you'll illustrate the value of each – which is what you are aiming to do with your CV.

See Appendix 2 for some examples of excellent and poor answers you could give on such a form.

Interviews

An interview is a performance. Your job as the interviewee is to keep your audience entertained and interested. If you do this, the odds are that you'll get the job: if you don't, you'll certainly get good, positive feedback and a sense that they would have hired you if only there hadn't been another candidate who was even stronger.

There's no magic formula to success at interview, but it's worth considering three things, in descending order of importance: the way you use your body, the way you use your voice, and what you say.

1. Body language

Eighty-five per cent of communication is non-verbal. This astonishes people, but it's true. What you look like and how you use your body are far, far more important that what you say. You need to create an impression of strength, reliability and trustworthiness. Here's a checklist of things to do.

- **Dress correctly**

Get the clothes right. Regardless of the company, dress smart – even if the people interviewing you are wearing jeans, you will create an impression of keenness – always a good thing. Men should wear a dark suit, with a dark tie and a light coloured shirt. Your suit and your shirt need to fit properly – make sure you are measured in a shop before buying anything. You should wear black – not brown – shoes, and they should be leather not suede. And they should be polished. Take out any earrings or piercings. Make sure your hair is neat. The world has changed and it's no longer the case that you have to shave off dreadlocks or cornrows to get a job – *so long as what you are wearing is impeccable and professional.*

Women should wear a dark business suit with a light-coloured shirt. Wear black heels or flats. Tie your hair back and keep make-up and jewellery to a minimum.

- **Smile!**

  It sounds so obvious – but wouldn't you rather work with someone smiley and pleasant than someone who constantly looks as if the world is out to get them? So would your interviewer. So from the moment you arrive, smile – smile at the receptionist, at other candidates and at the interviewers. You need to come across as a pleasant individual, and smiling is the easiest way to make sure this happens!

- **Posture**

  Imagine you're interviewing and you have two candidates, one slumped in his chair with his shoulders forward and his head down, and the other sitting straight up with her shoulders back and head up proudly. Who looks more reliable and trustworthy? Who looks keener? Who looks as if she'd be a better hire? Posture is important and it's easy to get it right – tuck your tummy in, put your shoulders back, hold your head up, and you're away.

- **Hands**

  Hands are really important. When you meet people, a firm handshake is critical – don't try and bear-hug their hands so that they need a trip to A&E to check nothing has been broken, but make sure you get a decent grip. And then when you talk, use your hands for emphasis – not obsessively, but when you are saying something especially important.

- **Eyes**

  Look your interviewer in the eye. Not the whole way

through, but certainly when you shake hands, and again at especially important points. Using eyes and hands together – i.e. making a hand gesture and simultaneously looking the interviewer in the eye – creates a very powerful impression.

- **Fiddling**

  Don't. Interviewing someone who is fiddling with something is incredibly annoying and makes it look as if you, the interviewee, are not giving their full attention. So remove all temptation – pens, watches, jewellery, dangling bits of hair – and if necessary sit with your hands clasped together.

- **Listen**

  Listen carefully to the questions that you get asked. Don't be afraid to pause and reflect before giving your answer. Or to ask for clarification if you aren't sure about the question. This makes you seem more thoughtful and attentive.

> *The Definitive Book of Body Language* by Allan and Barbara Pease has received good reviews and is worth checking out.

2. Voice

After becoming leader of the Conservative Party in 1975, Margaret Thatcher famously hired a voice coach to deepen her previously shrill tone. The whole image of the Iron Lady – an image which enabled her to break the trade unions, recapture the Falkland Islands and become Britain's longest-serving prime minister for two centuries – would not have worked without the deep, confident tone she acquired.

Believe it or not, the *sound* of your voice is considerably more important than what you actually say.

Fifteen years after Thatcher's departure, the Conservative Party found itself being led by Iain Duncan Smith. Duncan Smith was very quiet and, despite intensive coaching, his weak, faltering voice failed to resonate with his followers – he simply didn't sound like a leader, regardless of what he actually said, and almost from the start of his term there were whispers that he wasn't up to the job. At the Tory Party conference of 2003, Duncan Smith told followers not to 'underestimate the determination of a quiet man', but the whispers continued. Duncan Smith was doomed – and the party ditched him within one parliamentary term.

Thatcher's voice was a powerful tool, while Duncan Smith's was a terrible disadvantage. What each had to say mattered less than the way in which they said it. This is a powerful lesson: you need to use your voice as a weapon. Here are a few tips.

- **Volume**

  Vary the volume. To draw listeners in, speak quietly, and lean forward. If you need added emphasis, speak more loudly. Be conscious of your volume and use it as a tool.

- **Pace**

  Do not speak too quickly. One of the most common errors young people make is to garble their words, running them together in an attempt to say everything as quickly as possible. This is a bad idea. You need to make sure your listener can follow what you're saying – and you want to give him or her clues as to the really important bits – so *slow down* on those bits and give every word due emphasis. If you want a role model, listen to some of Barack Obama's speeches. His slow, rhythmic cadences emphasise every point he makes and lend him gravitas and credibility.

- **Pauses**

  The power of a pause is not to be underestimated. It's a good idea to sometimes pause after an especially tricky question, for thought – and to show your listener that you are reflective. It's also good to pause before making a really important point, for emphasis.

- **Tone**

  Listen to yourself speak. Does your voice go up at the end of a sentence, as if you were asking a question? It shouldn't – it should go down, as if you were saying something of which you were certain. Interviewers want you to be confident and certain rather than nervous and constantly seeking confirmation, so your tone must convey that impression. Again, you could do no better than to listen to Obama for an example.

- **Pitch**

  If you have a very high voice, try to lower it a bit – a very high pitch can be grating. And if your voice is very low, you might want to make it a bit higher – sounding like Barry White in an interview is not the best thing!

3. Content

This is what people invariably fixate on in an interview – what are they going to ask me? How should I answer? What you say is important, of course, and the next few pages deal in detail with those questions. But before proceeding, look again at the sections on body language and voice and realise that 85 per cent of your success or failure at interview will depend on them, rather than on what you actually say – so you would do well to spend some time practising the performance aspect of an interview as well as the actual content.

• Fundamentals

Fundamentally, the interviewer is going to want to know three things. Why do you want to do the job? What are your strengths? And what are your weaknesses?

So why *do* you want this job?

This is a very simple question – but a good answer is usually quite complicated. In order to say why you want the job, you need to say why you want that particular role, in that particular firm, in that particular industry. Real and lasting success comes when you match the values of the firm to your own ambitions and values – and that takes self-knowledge and real research. So to answer this question properly you'll have to talk at length about what you want from your career, and why this opportunity will provide it. You'll have to show real knowledge of the firm and its industry – and this probably means reading the relevant trade press (e.g. *PR Week* for PR; the *Bookseller* for publishing; *Accountancy Age* for accountancy, etc.) and talking to people who already work in the industry. Interviewers will be looking to see that your expectations are realistic and you know what you're applying for. Your job is to show that you really do want the role, and for the right reasons. Crucially, you must also show that you will add value to the company. A lot of interviewees go in with the attitude of 'What can this company do from me? How can I benefit from working here?' To paraphrase John F. Kennedy: *Ask not what your company can do for you, but what you can do for your company.*

- **Strengths**

  They'll ask – in one way or another – what your strengths are. You need to know yourself in order to be able to give an honest and realistic answer to this question. And you need to support what you say with examples. No one has ever claimed to an interviewer that they are lazy, dishonest and incompetent – so rather than just telling them about how hard-working, honest and competent you are, you need to give some examples (probably from your extra-curricular work or work experience).

- **Weaknesses**

  They'll also probably ask what your weaknesses are, or which areas you might need particular support in. This is a good question which tests your self-knowledge and your honesty. My advice is that you tell the truth, but sugar the pill by also saying – unprompted – what you are doing to address these weaknesses. For example, let's imagine you're going for a job as a management consultant but you have studied history: 'I'm not as commercially aware as people who are perhaps studying for a more commercial degree. But I know this is a problem, so I have taken to reading the *FT* every day and *The Economist* every week, and I'm building up my business knowledge that way.'

- **Competency-based questions**

  Here are some of the questions you are likely to face. They are divided into sections, with notes on each. Remember, the best idea is to answer with reference to a range of experiences – previous paid work, work placements and extra-curricular activities. Avoid academic examples if you can – they tend to be things you had to do, rather than things you chose to do, so they don't make you stand out. You want to give the impression that you have done a variety of interesting and useful things, so don't fall into the trap of letting all your examples come from one or two specific episodes in your life.

  – **Motivation**

    What attracted you to this company, and to this role specifically?

    Why do you want to work in investment banking/consultancy/advertising, etc?

    What other applications have you made?

    What's different about this role?

    What skills could you bring to the role above anyone else?

    What areas do you think you would need particular support in?

Tell me about an initiative you've had to work hard to drive through. How did you sell it to others? What specific hurdles did you have to overcome?

What do you read?

These questions are aiming to place you in context. Where are you coming from? What do you want from your life? What are you good and bad at? Why do you want to do this job?

– **Planning and organisation**

Describe a major project you've been involved with and your role in this project.

What has been the toughest project/work you've been asked to do?

Give me an example of a time when you've made a mistake. How did you react? What did you do?

Give me an example of meeting a deadline

These questions are specifically designed to produce evidence of your ability to plan and organise. You need to answer honestly, but artfully: give examples of things that you've done well.

– **Initiative**

Describe a time when you've had to rely on your own initiative.

Give me an example of a time when you've had to improve an existing work process or procedure.

How much of a self-starter are you? Can you give a good example of setting up a system yourself?

- **Resourcefulness**

Give me an example of when your plans have been totally disrupted by an unexpected event. What was your first reaction? What did you do about it?

Describe a time when you've had to stick up for your own views against a more senior person. How did you feel? Tell me what was said. What would you do differently in retrospect?

Describe a time when you have lost your cool about something at work. How did you react; what did you do?

Tell me about a recent situation when you've had to make an on-the-spot decision. What would have happened if you had not acted?

Describe a time when you have had to find answers to questions without help from others.

*How do you deal with adversity? A recent and influential HR book (*Topgrading: How Leading Companies Win by Hiring, Coaching, and Keeping the Best People* by Bradford D. Smart) described resourcefulness as the 'supercompetency'. You have to have compelling examples of times when you have been resilient and resourceful.*

– **Interpersonal skills**

Tell me about a recent situation in which you've disagreed with a colleague. How did you deal with it? What was the outcome?

Tell me about a situation in which you've felt intimidated by someone at work. Why did you feel this way? How did you cope with it?

Tell me about a time when you've had to motivate others. How did you communicate your enthusiasm? How did they react to you?

What sorts of people do you find more difficult to work with/relate to? What did you do to enable you to build a better relationship with them?

Can you work with other people? How do you handle conflict? Are you a closet sociopath, or will you fit nicely into the team?

– **Sharing knowledge/networks**

Describe how you have set up internal/external networks. How has this been beneficial? Who are your main contacts?

Do you understand the power of networking – and are you any good at it?

– **Communication**

Tell me about the most difficult presentation you've made. Why was it particularly difficult? How happy did you feel afterwards about your performance?

Tell me about how you've explained and organised a specific project. What guidelines did you give? Who planned the project? How did you monitor its progress?

Under what circumstances do you think you communicate most effectively? Why in these circumstances? What affects your communication adversely?

Tell me about the last time someone came to you for guidance/support. How did you deal with this situation? Do you think the employee/colleague benefited from your guidance?

Tell me about a recent experience when you gave support to an individual, What advice did you offer? What would you do differently in retrospect?

What was the worst relationship you've ever had with a colleague? Why was it so bad? How did you try to improve it? Were you successful?

How do you demonstrate respect for others' opinions?

Describe to me how you normally interact with people at work. How do others respond to you?

Describe a time when you've accepted some else's idea because it was better than yours.

How able are you to communicate to different audiences? Have you grasped the idea that communication is a two-way process – involving listening as well as talking?

– **Flexibility/influences**

Tell me about a situation in which you've disagreed with others. Did you manage to persuade them to your way of thinking? What was the outcome?

Describe a situation in which you've changed your style or approach in order to influence someone. What did you do?

In what role have you had to be extremely flexible in approach?

How good are you at getting others to do what you want, and how flexible are you in the way that you do things?

Assessment centres

Some employers, following an initial interview, will invite successful candidates to an assessment centre. These sessions usually last for half a day or a whole day – and occasionally for two days. There will be a variety of exercises, but they might include: a maths test, a reading or writing test, a psychometric test, presentations, group exercises and more individual interviews. There may well be a lunch or dinner with other candidates and assessors too.

These are the key rules for success at assessment centres:

- Listen. And use body language to show that you are listening.
- When you have something to say, ensure that you speak up in a confident and assertive manner, and that your voice is heard.
- If you find that people aren't listening, point out, politely, that you have something to say that may benefit the group.
- Include the excluded ('What do you think?'), and make sure that everyone else listens.
- If alcohol is available, don't drink it. Having a drink may make you feel more comfortable, but it also makes you more likely to say something silly.
- Initiate conversations, both with other candidates and with the company's staff. Ask them questions, and listen to the answers!
- Be polite to *everyone* – including receptionists, secretaries, etc. We know of more than one case where individuals who have aced an assessment centre have not got job offers because of rudeness to people doing 'menial' jobs.

Networking

One of the things that distinguishes people who have real and lasting success in their careers is a really strong network. A network, at its best, can provide you with mentoring, inspiration, emotional support, financial support, the opportunity to learn, the opportunity to teach, and the opportunity to help and to be helped. The central principle of networking is the same as the central principle of any human relationship: to treat others as you would like them to treat you.

Creating a network

How exactly do you go about creating a network? There are two key elements – proactiveness and receptiveness.

Proactiveness means actively seeking out people with whom you would like to have contact. You attend seminars, lectures and events, and you ask questions, introduce yourself to people, take their cards and drop them an email afterwards to say how nice it was to meet them. If you think it would be useful to talk to them some more, ask them out for coffee or lunch; if you want something from them, ask. People who are good networkers usually say yes.

Receptiveness means that when people ask you to network, you say yes. It could be a younger person from school or university who wants advice; it could be the brother or sister or friend of a friend; it could even be an older person who has taken a shine to you and wants to help. Regardless, the trick is always to be pleasant and courteous and to give up some of your time for others.

Key people

Once you have a network, the trick is not just to use it but to leverage it – in other words, to use it to your advantage. An exercise worth doing once every twelve months or so is this: write a list of all the people you know – everyone. Then mark out on the list those people that you think can help you in your career. You should make it your business to stay in touch with these Key People – the occasional card or letter or coffee or lunch will do the trick – even if you don't see how they can help you immediately: because the day will come when they can help you, and if you have a strong relationship, you'll be in a much better position to get that help.

This is not, of course, to suggest that you should ignore everyone else in your network; far from it. There will be people you especially like, and with whom you make an effort to stay in touch, simply because of the pleasure you take in their company; there will be other people who you are committed to helping, too. But the point of defining Key People is to know exactly who you *have* to keep in touch with.

Use what you've got

In life, everyone is dealt a different hand. Sometimes it can feel as if other people hold the aces while you're left with terrible cards. But the fact of the matter is, everyone is unique, and there are always ways you can leverage your uniqueness – or, in simple language, use what you've got. Here's a case study.

Ekow Eshun is a former creative director of the Institute

of Contemporary Art, and a successful novelist, broadcaster and journalist. Before that, at the age of 29 Ekow became editor of *Arena*, and the youngest-ever editor of a men's magazine. I remember hearing him talk once about how he did this, and his words have stayed with me ever since. Essentially, growing up, Ekow was obsessed with trainers. He had dozens of pairs and he was always interested in what people were wearing. His mother would frequently tell him off for spending so much time obsessing about something useless – but he didn't care. As he grew older and got to university, it occurred to him that a teenage obsession could become something more. After all, there were journalists who actually got *paid* to write about trainers. And he almost certainly knew more than them. So he looked at the latest trends and noticed – this was the late 1980s – that more and more people were wearing Kickers, a hitherto very unfashionable brand. Figuring he had nothing to lose, he sent a very brief, 100-word article to *The Face*. They ran it. None of their regular contributors had noticed how cool Kickers were becoming, and he had. It was a humble, unsolicited (and unpaid) start, but he was still a student, and he had his first article in a national magazine.

Integrity and communication

I urge you in the strongest possible terms to behave with honour, dignity and integrity at all times. Specifically, you should follow these three golden rules:

- Always, always, always be on time. I recommend aiming to turn up for interviews one hour early, making sure you have the right place, and then going round the corner and having a cup of tea for an hour before turning up bang on time. Do not be more than a few minutes early and do not, whatever you do, ever be late.

- Never make a promise you can't keep. For example, don't promise to take a job that you're unsure about, and then renege: instead, say that you are flattered by the offer but need a little time to decide.

- If you have to withdraw from an application process or decline a job offer, do so with the utmost courtesy and honesty. Never fall into the trap of thinking that you can behave badly because you don't want to work for a particular person or firm. People move jobs, your career develops, and you never know what's round the corner – you should treat people as you would like to be treated yourself.

- Finally, you should know the power of an apology. If for whatever reason you fail to keep to any of these golden rules, you should have the self-confidence and integrity to apologise to the person concerned. You never know when you might run into them again or who they might talk to, and you should acknowledge that your usual standards have not been met and say sorry.

CONCLUSIONS

You are talented, intelligent and resourceful. This is a good starting point. The fact that you are reading this already shows that you are prepared to go the extra mile and do the extra research to ensure that you land the job you want.

There will always be competition for top jobs, and at the time of writing the economy is faltering, which means that this competition is getting more intense. It's important therefore that during the process of job-hunting, and also well in advance, you leave as little as possible to chance, and do all that's required to ensure that you have the edge over those you are competing with.

- You:
  - Believe in yourself
  - Are not a victim
  - Are not afraid of failure, but are realistic about potential setbacks
  - Are a Strategist.

- You have:
  - Set realistic goals to match your personality and your style of working
  - Researched the fields you are interested in
  - Thought about your initial choices.

- You will:
  - Tailor your application to the job you're going for
  - Make sure your CV and application form are well presented or correctly filled out
  - Prepare for the interview
  - Work on your body language.

- And finally you:
  - Are presentable and impeccably turned out
  - Use your interpersonal skills to build up a network
  - Make the best use of your existing knowledge and skills
  - Behave with honour, integrity and dignity at all times.

The main thing to remember is that if you do your research, are committed, well prepared and focused, then you *will* succeed. And perhaps some day soon young people at the start of their career will be coming for advice to you, a successful and respected professional in your chosen field.

APPENDIX 1

A killer CV

This is an example of an excellent CV. Note in particular:

- The layout, which is clean, simple and consistent.
- The way Jane explains and contextualises each of her achievements.
- The way she makes even routine retail work seem impressive: 'I constantly exceeded my targets.'

JANE HILL

D.O.B: 15/07/90 **Nationality:** British
Address: 81 Beaconsfield Road, London SE27 8AW
Mobile: 07912 34567 **Email:** jhill333@warwick.ac.uk

Education:

University of Warwick (2008–present)
BSc Economics

Richmond-Upon-Thames Sixth Form College (2006–2008)
3 A-levels: Mathematics (A), Economics (A), Chemistry (A)
3 AS-levels: Philosophy of Religion (A), Accounting (A), Further Maths (A)

St Martin's-in-the-Fields High School for Girls (2004–2006)
10 GCSEs: 5 A*s, 2 As, 3 Bs

Work experience:

Olivier Johnson & Co., Registered Auditors & Tax Consultants

July 2009–present

- Accurately processing staff payroll on a monthly and weekly basis using accounting software such as Sage payroll and IRIS PAYE
- Ensuring payroll system set up correctly – inputting personnel changes
- Working closely with other accounts personnel
- Maintenance of petty cash
- Learnt how to use other accounting software such as Sage Accounts and IRIS Book-keeping

H. Samuel, Victoria, London

July–September 2007

- Worked on the tills and handled large amounts of money
- Developed negotiation and persuasion skills as I had to find solutions to customers' problems while handling customer requests and complaints
- Learnt to remain calm and efficient under pressure when working as a member of a team and meeting store targets; achieved employee of the week within first couple of weeks of employment as I constantly exceeded my targets

Taplow Pharmacy, Woolwich, London

July–August 2006

- Used my initiative when dealing with errors pertaining to customers' prescriptions and when performing general retail tasks; developed a method of managing prescriptions which was more efficient than previous method
- Developed my communication skills by learning to deal with customers with tact and diplomacy

Arabic Bank PLC, Moorgate, London
June–July 2005

- Worked in the Corporate and Institutional Banking department with experiences in Syndicated Loans and Property Finance

- Gained experience in working within a team, which involves compromise, commitment, planning, organisation and time management
- Gained analytic and diagnostic skills, which helped me to complete the tasks I was given; developed a system of organising clients' documents, which ensured that documents could be extracted with ease
- Performed a series of administrative and accounting functions within the Finance Department

Positions of responsibility:

- Course representative of the Student–Staff Liaison Committee – this has aided my communication skills; I have driven positive changes in my faculty in relation to methods of assessment and student–staff relationships.
- Member of the communication team of Warwick International Development Society – this has aided my networking and teamwork skills as we arrange talks for our annual summit and invite speakers from all over the world to discuss international development issues.
- One of the leaders of my church youth committee – I coordinate and motivate large groups of young people towards achieving our clearly defined goals; organising youth concerts and youth events. I make difficult and sometimes costly judgements when it is necessary. This has allowed me to develop my leadership and organisational skills as well as learning to deal with different types of people and ensuring that everything is working as efficiently as it should be.
- Academic mentor for Warwick Volunteers – I have built relationships and learnt to be extremely committed to the young ladies I mentor. I approach their problems in a personal and creative manner and think on my feet when necessary. I motivate them to believe they can achieve their goals and guide them in the process of achieving them.
- I have a proven interest in finance. Since starting university I have attended the Pricewaterhouse Cooper School Leaver Open Day, the Accenture Undergraduate Insight Day, the UBS Focus on Finance seminars and the Merrill Lynch Skills for Success Workshop.

Extra-curricular activities and interests:

- Economics Society (Social Secretary of the society)
- Linguistic Improvement and Practice Society
- Eastern Food Appreciation Society
- Afro-Caribbean Society
- Nigerian Society (Treasurer of the society)
- Christian Union; Revelation Rock – Gospel Choir
- French language course with Alfred Academy, Perpignan, France

Additional skills:

- **IT skills** – I have achieved Level 3 Key Skills in ICT; I am competent in a number of IT packages such as MS Word, MS Excel, MS Access, MS PowerPoint and Internet Explorer among others. I am also competent in accounting packages such as Sage.
- **Language skills**: French – Basic; Yoruba – Fluent

Referees:

Mr Gene Simmons CBE (personal tutor)
Warwick University
Warwick WX1 1DW

Ms Alice Cooper (branch manager)
H. Samuel, Victoria
London E1N 8B3

APPENDIX 2

Filling out competency-based forms

Typically, an application form consists of filling in basic personal information (name, address, grades, etc.) and then answering several motivational or competency-based questions.

Always make sure that you follow the laid-out guidelines. When answering questions:

1. Know your goal.
2. Avoid mistakes.
3. Omit needless words.
4. Avoid unnecessarily long sentences.
5. Avoid the passive voice.
6. Use simple language.
7. Use the appropriate register.
8. Support your assertions.

You should also always write to or near the word limit. If there is no limit stated, then write a substantial amount – 600 words approximately.

Here are some typical questions and some model (and not so model!) answers.

1. Please describe why you have chosen to apply to UBS

Model answer

I first decided to apply for UBS after attending the QS Women in Leadership Forum, where I met a number of UBS representatives. I got on very well with them and I was impressed by what they told me of the entrepreneurial nature of the firm. I also learnt about the Explore training programme.

A strong training programme is essential at this starting point of my career and I think that the internship programme will offer me a full understanding of the firm by giving me a thorough initial orientation and extensive training before letting me do relevant work. Doing relevant work will give me the chance to really experience what it is like to work for UBS, while the many networking opportunities with current employees will give me the chance to find out about working in all areas of the firm, and to focus my ideas of which area would be best for me.

Should I subsequently gain employment with UBS, the 18–24 month Explore programme will ensure that I succeed. Encouraging graduate hires to set objectives for their training early on means that I will be able to increase the value of the subsequent training. The Ready-for-work training will get us ready to move onto our desks, by giving us the essential knowledge needed for the job. Once we progress onto our desks, we learn while doing useful work, and the mentorship programme is a great way to ensure that we don't get lost. Further training schemes give us the chance to fulfill our initial aims. The many networking opportunities are fun and are also a great way to meet other interns and to develop a network of contacts within UBS who can help us work more effectively.

I was pleased to see that professional development doesn't end with the end of the Explore programme. There are opportunities to refresh old skills or learn new ones from the ongoing courses to more focused programmes. The Essential Management Skills course caught my eye as the ideal way to ensure that employees are able to deal with more senior positions, while the Accelerated Leadership Experience for mid-level managers looks like something to aim to be involved in some years in the future.

The importance that UBS places on training was demonstrated to me by the fact that training was mentioned in the 2006 annual report, in the context of new joiners who had previously worked at CERN. This appealed to me as it showed that the work at UBS was intellectually challenging enough for former scientists to be kept interested while the training programme is good enough to deal with a significant change in career paths.

Attending the UBS presentation at my university demonstrated to me the global reach of UBS. Unlike some banks UBS has a strong presence in both Europe and the Americas (39% and 51%) as well as a strong presence in emerging markets, as demonstrated by the firm winning 'Best Global Emerging Markets Investment Bank' from Euro Money *this year. This puts UBS in an ideal position to respond to changes in world markets.*

Talking to more senior employees of the firm at the university presentation I was impressed by the entrepreneurial spirit of the firm and how it works with employees to create the most productive working conditions. These conditions together will make UBS an inspirational and educational place to work.

Julie Chakraverty, Global Head of Client Analytics and Connectivity, Global COO for Client Coverage and head of the women's network at UBS, particularly inspired me to apply. I met her after she gave a talk at the QS Women in Leadership forum. I was impressed both by her speech and how willing she was to take time out of her busy schedule to do an interview for the student magazine that I am involved with.

This is an excellent answer. It is detailed and specific, loaded with genuine analysis and informed opinions based on facts. It is simply written and easy to read.

Now turn the page for an example of the wrong sort of answer.

1. Please describe why you have chosen to apply to UBS

Poor answer

UBS represents the benchmark in a fiercely competitive global industry and I would be honoured to commance my career in banking within this organisatianal structure. UBS is a global and multicultural powerhouse institution that prides itself on a collegiate, yet critical, corporate culture. Twinned with positive momentum even amidst the current depressing market energy, UBS maintains its confidence and focuses on increasing its market share. This confidence is exuded by the corporate culture, which filters down at each individual, as past experience within the organisation has taught me.

My involvement in the 'Brokerage Citylink' internship gave me a platform to immerse myself in the real vibrant culture at UBS. Never have I been so astounded and proud to be a part of an innovative team that actually lives up to all of its formally set standards. Diversaty, camaraderie, and responsibility are mere assertions made by most in this industry, but at UBS, I found these to be an actuality that was studiously radiated by all employees throughout the organisation.

It is for the aforementioned reasons, coupled with UBS' consistent growth and high business confidence, that I believe this institution provides the best platform for junior bankers as myself to take a bigger step in the investment banking arena.

This is a very poor answer. It's too short and riddled with basic errors of spelling and grammar. There are no hard facts whatsoever – just wishy-washy opinions backed up by nothing. The answer is generic and could refer to any bank. Ask yourself – would you hire this person?

2. Why did you choose the specific business area to which you have applied? Why do you think you will succeed in this area?

Model answer

I am interested in the FI&MCC division of UBS because it will give me the opportunity to work with tangible products within the financial arena. I am excited by the prospect of dealing with products such as sugar, milk or even pork bellies that are used by the average household. I have developed a real hunger for the commodities market in the past year and have immersed myself in publications such as the Financial Times *and* The Economist. *I would love the opportunity to be at the forefront of the commodities industry; the chance to be a player in the global markets and not merely a bystander reading about key market movements hours after they have take place.*

Moreover, I would like to work in an area of the bank that uses a great deal of macroeconomic analysis, as this is the branch of economics that I am particularly interested in. The challenge of analysing the close relationship between changes in macro-economic variables such as interest rate movements and developments within the fixed income and commodities markets is very appealing to me. The recent decline in the value of the dollar has also captured my attention in recent weeks. The fall in the greenback owing to various factors, such as fears about the state of the US economy, and a resultant potential reduction in the Federal Reserve rates have had a direct impact on the prices of commodities such as gold, which has risen from just under $650 per troy ounce at the start of 2007 to the mid-$800 region in recent months. The appreciation in gold prices, that has seen it reach 28-year record *highs, is largely a result of an increase in demand from investors seeking a safe haven from the US dollar. This exemplifies the interconnectedness of macroeconomic variables and commodity prices, which contributes to my immense fascination with the market.*

The susceptibility of many areas of the commodities market to changes in the political climate is also very appealing. This aspect of the industry will enable me to apply some of the knowledge and analysis of international politics which I have developed over the course of my degree. In this instance, I would cite the example of the recent surge in oil prices that ensued from the ongoing geo-political tension between Iran and Turkey. This, coupled with the more recent fears about US inventory levels, has contributed to the ascent of oil prices towards the $100 level. On a more sentimental note, as a Nigerian-born person, I am continuously expanding my interest in developments within the oil industry; I would seize any opportunity to conduct further research and analysis into the industry that accounts for approximately 84% of my home nation's major exports. I would be fascinated to analyse the extent to which continuous struggles in the oil-rich Delta region affect the national and more particularly global output of oil.

My internship within the Fixed Income and Commodities division of a competitor firm gave me a first hand insight into this side of the banking industry. During this experience, I was charged with the responsibility of conducting research on a range of energy exchanges. Although I was dealing with companies and products that I was not entirely familiar with, I was able to meet the challenge of producing a comprehensive report on my findings. Moreover, I thoroughly enjoyed the challenge and the experience served to increase my desire to pursue a career within this sector.

I believe I will succeed in this role because I have the necessary skills and persona that are required to thrive within the FI&MCC division of UBS. These factors have been developed by the number of activities that I take part in; my participation in college sport teams has developed my team work skills, whilst my aptitude in leadership roles has been heightened by my role within my community group. These skills are further enhanced by my personal drive and insatiable yearning to succeed.

A superb answer. The writer breaks his answer into two distinct parts – and spends more time showing off his knowledge of the role than talking about his personal qualities. The answer is brimming with hard facts, detail and analysis. Clearly, the writer knows what he is talking about and has an overwhelming enthusiasm for the role.

Now turn the page for an example of a poor answer to the same question.

2. Why did you choose the specific business area to which you have applied? Why do you think you will succeed in this area?

Poor answer

I have chosen the investment banking business group because I am interested in following a career as an investment banker but I would like to gain work experience that allows me to rotate thorough the different divisions so that I can find out which division I would be best suited to. This is why I have chosen to apply to the investment banking business area rather than a specialist area such as fix income and money market trading. I feel that I will be well suited to this specific area because I am an individual who is willing to learn and willing to work extremely hard at any task that is presented to me. This is evident throughout my academic background, where I have shown consistency in achievement. Outside of education, evidence of my strong work ethic can be seen through my part-time work experience with the housing benefit team. Initially when I joined the team the department experienced a back lodge of thousands of claims. I had to work in conjunction with a small group of individuals who substantially reduced the back lodge over a period of months. Towards the latter stages of summer I also worked at my local Tesco supermarket and held two jobs at the same time. I believe that I will prosper in this division because I enjoy solving problems and I am able to persevere through problems until I reach the solution. This is an integral part of my degree discipline and I feel that this experience is essential, irrespective of the division I work in. I also enjoy to communicate and interact with others. I am a social person who is involved in team activities and creative pursuits such as;

playing basketball and hosting a weekly radio show, as described earlier in my application form. These activities allow me to build confidence skills that will be useful when presenting ideas to clients and also exercise my creativity in problem solving.

Very weak. There are basic errors again ('fix income' and 'back lodge', for example), and a total lack of hard detail on what actually happens in the writer's area. The writer gives reasonable detail about herself but offers no real facts on the position she's applying for.

3. Describe the achievement of which you are most proud

Model answer

The achievement of which I am most proud is when I was chosen to represent the UK in Johns Hopkins University aged thirteen. I was flown to Baltimore, to participate in a three-week long course in mathematical reasoning. It was not the first time I had ever travelled to America, but it was the first time I had ever left this country on my own. Living in America for such a long period, whilst being on an intensive programme on my own, was a big challenge.

Not only were the culture, language and weather different, but the material being covered on the course was radically different from school mathematics and was being taught using methods I had never experienced. Not one to be fazed by this, I soldiered on, making major differences to the way I thought about certain mathematical questions and wrote down my answers. I also had to acclimatise to the ideas introduced for conducting extensive online research, consulting encyclopaedic publications and using the university's vast library to find journals in the relevant section. This broadened my horizons academically and expanded both my vocabulary and knowledge rapidly.

The same was true inside the classroom. Being the youngest person on my course and one of only three girls in a class of twenty was also initially very daunting. The material being covered was proving difficult for all of the older boys as it was totally unfamiliar to them. This was also true for me, but I learnt to cope with both the pace and depth of the ideas explored. At times I was even able to transfer knowledge I had acquired whilst studying for A-level mathematics and relate it to concepts being covered. Many times this gave me an advantage over all of the other students in the class and impressed our lecturers!

There were also challenges to be experienced outside the classroom. Being the only child, out of close to six hundred children, who had a British accent also caused problems as a lot of what I said to the other children had to be repeated. Though a small stumbling block, at times this did become rather frustrating as did the challenge of eating 'American' food. A daily helping of hamburgers and French fries was a far cry from English school lunches with sandwiches, pasta and salad bars. Being so far away from my family and our meals together was another challenge I had to overcome.

The whole experience made me a more independent and confident person and I learnt a lot of new and advanced mathematical ideas that I did not encounter formally until I started University last year. I still find myself relying on lessons learnt that summer when trying to settle into University life here at Oxford.

This is an exceptional answer. The writer tells a fascinating and deeply personal story. On another level, she relates her experience in such a way as to show the best of her personal qualities. There is great depth here and not a trace of cliché.

A poor answer to the same question follows on the next page.

3. Describe the achievement of which you are most proud

Poor answer

In 2001, I relocated to England from Nigeria. Being my first time abroad, it was a challenge settling down as I had to get accustomed to the British lifestyle and the drastic change of weather. I also had to settle into a new education system. However the education system in Nigeria was an advantage in certain aspects. I strived for academic excellence and gained a successful application to study A levels at Tiffin Girls' School after my GCSEs at a comprehensive school and a year ago gained admission into London School of Economics to study for a degree in Accounting & Finance. Also being elected as a society representative has proved really worthwhile as I am able to put the knowledge gained so far in my degree into practice. These transitions in life have made me more adaptable.

Weak. There is no narrative here, and the writer has not answered the question – she has simply listed a series of (fairly standard) achievements. There is nothing here to make a recruiter *want* to meet this person.

ACKNOWLEDGEMENTS

Thanks are due to Paul Forty, Daniel Mokades, and Anton Shelupanov for all their help and advice with the production of this book.

For more information about Raphael's company,
Rare Recruitment, please visit www.rarerecruitment.co.uk